This book belongs to:

_____

_____

A Note to Parents and Teachers

This book offers you a wonderful opportunity to enter the world of Christmas with your children. The illustrations and simple text provide an introduction to the Christmas story, but I encourage you to sit down and slowly read the Gospel accounts of the birth of Jesus with your little ones.

Children may also enjoy acting out the scenes of *A Christmas Interview* as a play, singing their favorite Christmas carols as they go along.

Father Yoshiike

A Christmas Interview

Reporting Live from Bethlehem!

Written by
Father Yoshitaka Yoshiike

Illustrated by
Fujio Tsuchiya

Pauline
BOOKS & MEDIA
Boston

The two reporters arrive at the stable in the small town of Bethlehem.
Baby Jesus is sleeping in the manger.
Mary and Joseph are with him.
So are the shepherds and the Wise Men.

"Could you please tell us how you feel right now?"

"Relieved! I could not even find a room for Mary and me to stay in. That's why we're here in this stable. But now, as the angel had told us, God's Son has really been born!"

"An angel told you that?"

"Yes. Before Mary and I got married, I had a dream. And in my dream, an angel told me…"

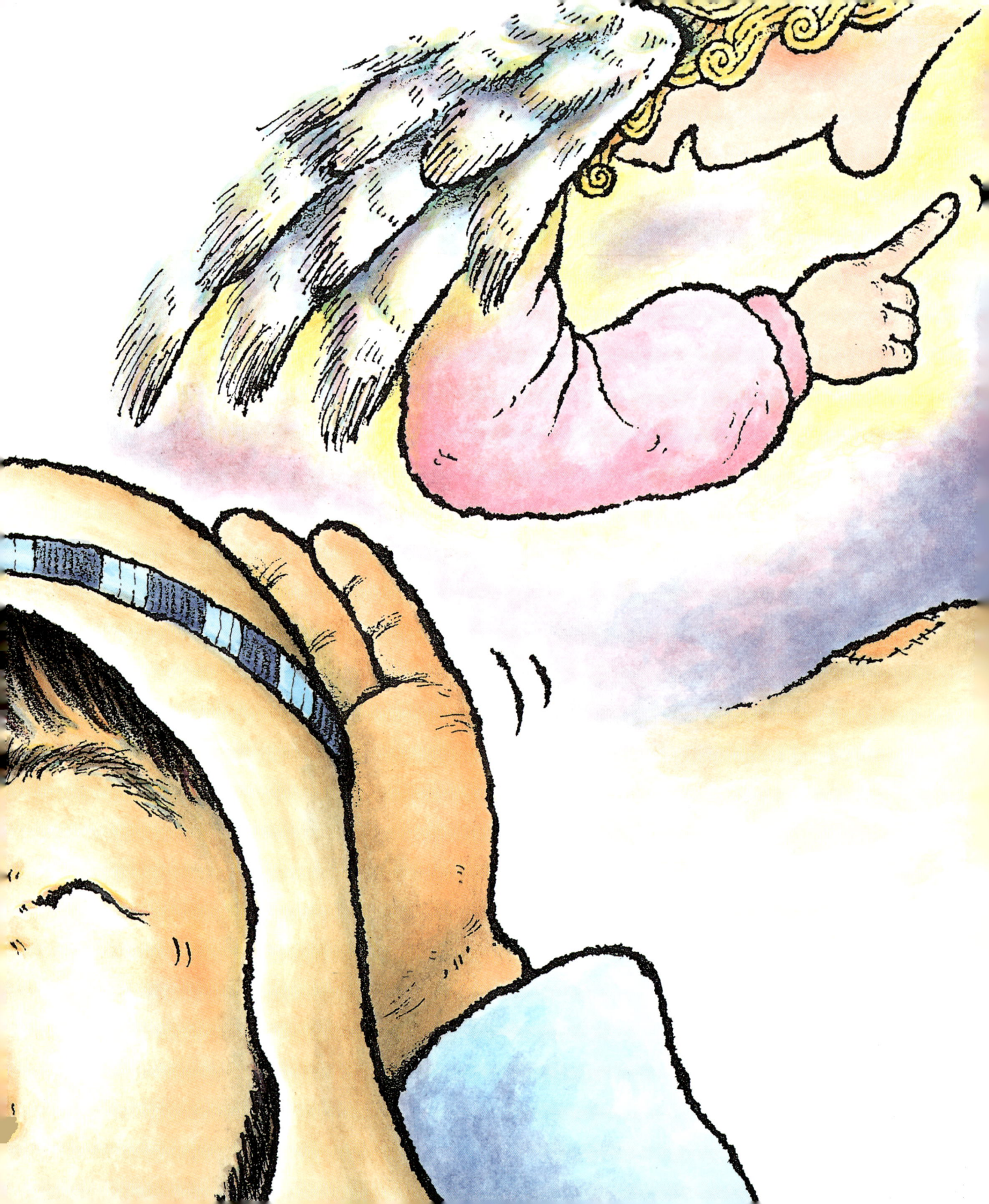

"'Do not be afraid, Joseph!
Mary will be the mother of the Savior,
and you will name him Jesus.'

"I believed what the angel said.
And now, God's Son, who will save the whole world,
has come to us as a little baby in a manger.
Isn't it amazing?"

"Mary, we know that an angel also visited you before Jesus was born.
What did the angel say?"

"The angel said,

'Be happy, Mary!
God has chosen you.
You will be the mother of Jesus,
God's own Son.
This will happen by the power
of the Holy Spirit.'

"Then I told the angel,
'I will do whatever God wants.'"

"You stay up all night
watching your sheep, right?
Can you tell us why you are here tonight?"

"Well, this is what happened. All of a sudden, in the middle of the night, we saw an angel. A bright light was shining all around us. Then the angel said, 'Here is good news for you! A Savior is born in Bethlehem!'

"We hurried to find the place where the Savior was. And we ended up here."

"We have a question for you, too.
What made you come all the way to Bethlehem?"

"In a faraway country, we saw a mysterious star.
We studied the star. We found out that it
meant that a Savior had been born."

"We decided to follow the star and come and adore the Savior."

"We'd like to interview Jesus,
of course, but he is too little.
He does look very happy, though.
Do you know why?"

Library of Congress Cataloging-in-Publication Data

Yoshiike, Y. (Yoshitaka)
  A Christmas interview : reporting live from Bethlehem! / written by Y. Yoshiike ; illustrated by Fujio Tsuchiya.—1st English ed.
     p. cm.
  ISBN 0-8198-1572-1 (pbk.)
  1. Jesus Christ—Nativity—Juvenile literature. I. Tsuchiya, Fujio. II. Title.
  BT315.3.Y67 2005
  232.92—dc22

                            2004025437

English adaptation by Patricia Edward Jablonski, FSP

Originally published in Japanese under the title *Chrismas Interview* by the Daughters of St. Paul, 12-42 Akasaka 8 Chome, Minatoku, Tokyo 107-0052

First English Edition, 2005

All rights reserved. No part of this book may be reproduced or transmitted in any form or by any means, electronic or mechanical, including photocopying, recording, or by any information storage and retrieval system without permission in writing from the publisher.

"P" and PAULINE are registered trademarks of the Daughters of St. Paul

Copyright © 2003, Yoshitaka Yoshiike & Fujio Tsuchiya / Joshi Pauro Kai (Daughters of St. Paul) Tokyo

Published by Pauline Books & Media, 50 Saint Paul's Avenue, Boston, MA 02130-3491.

Printed in Canada

www.pauline.org

Pauline Books & Media is the publishing house of the Daughters of St. Paul, an international congregation of women religious serving the Church with the communications media.

1 2 3 4 5 6 7 8 9   11 10 09 08 07 06 05

Pauline
BOOKS & MEDIA

The Daughters of St. Paul operate book and media centers at the following addresses. Visit, call or write the one nearest you today, or find us on the World Wide Web, www.pauline.org

CALIFORNIA	3908 Sepulveda Blvd, Culver City, CA 90230	310-397-8676
	5945 Balboa Avenue, San Diego, CA 92111	858-565-9181
	46 Geary Street, San Francisco, CA 94108	415-781-5180
FLORIDA	145 S.W. 107th Avenue, Miami, FL 33174	305-559-6715
HAWAII	1143 Bishop Street, Honolulu, HI 96813	808-521-2731
	Neighbor Islands call:	866-521-2731
ILLINOIS	172 North Michigan Avenue, Chicago, IL 60601	312-346-4228
LOUISIANA	4403 Veterans Memorial Blvd, Metairie, LA 70006	504-887-7631
MASSACHUSETTS	885 Providence Hwy, Dedham, MA 02026	781-326-5385
MISSOURI	9804 Watson Road, St. Louis, MO 63126	314-965-3512
NEW JERSEY	561 U.S. Route 1, Wick Plaza, Edison, NJ 08817	732-572-1200
NEW YORK	150 East 52nd Street, New York, NY 10022	212-754-1110
	78 Fort Place, Staten Island, NY 10301	718-447-5071
PENNSYLVANIA	9171-A Roosevelt Blvd, Philadelphia, PA 19114	215-676-9494
SOUTH CAROLINA	243 King Street, Charleston, SC 29401	843-577-0175
TENNESSEE	4811 Poplar Avenue, Memphis, TN 38117	901-761-2987
TEXAS	114 Main Plaza, San Antonio, TX 78205	210-224-8101
VIRGINIA	1025 King Street, Alexandria, VA 22314	703-549-3806
CANADA	3022 Dufferin Street, Toronto, Ontario, Canada M6B 3T5	416-781-9131

¡También somos su fuente para libros, videos y música en español!